YOUR MOTHER CALLED, AGAIN

160 QUIPS AND BARBS
FROM EVERYONE'S FAVORITE CRITIC

Your Mother Called, Again

13-Digit ISBN: 978-1-60433-960-4
10-Digit ISBN: 1-60433-960-8

This book may be ordered by mail from the publisher. Please include $5.99 for
postage and handling. Please support your local bookseller first!
Books published by Cider Mill Press Book Publishers are available at special
discounts for bulk purchases in the United States by corporations, institutions,
and other organizations. For more information, please contact the publisher.

Cider Mill Press Book Publishers
"Where good books are ready for press"
PO Box 454
12 Spring Street
Kennebunkport, Maine 04046
Visit us online!
cidermillpress.com

Typography: Adobe Garamond, BodoniFB, Clarendon,
Futura, Hanley Sans, Helvetica, Industry Inc.

Printed in China
1 2 3 4 5 6 7 8 9 0
First Edition

YOUR MOTHER CALLED, AGAIN

160 QUIPS AND BARBS
FROM EVERYONE'S FAVORITE CRITIC

JOHN BRUECKNER

CIDER MILL
PRESS

BOOK
PUBLISHERS
KENNEBUNKPORT, MAINE

CALL ME WHEN YOU GET THERE SO I KNOW YOU'RE SAFE. I KNOW WHEN YOU'RE LYING TO ME! "I DON'T KNOW" IS NOT AN ANSWER. I HOPE YOU DON'T KISS ME WITH THAT MOUTH! I NEED YOUR PROBLEMS LIKE I NEED A HOLE IN MY HEAD. I NEVER WOULD HAVE SPOKEN TO MY MOTHER LIKE THAT! YOU'D FORGET YOUR HEAD IF IT WASN'T ATTACHED TO YOUR SHOULDERS! YOU MADE YOUR BED, NOW GO LIE IN IT. YOU WON'T BE HAPPY UNTIL YOU BREAK THAT. WILL YOU

Contents

Introduction
"Uh-oh, it's Mom."

Those dreaded words can strike fear into any child. Who knows what Mom has in store for you now? A phone call from her can feel like an interrogation, a game of 20 Questions with your life as the subject. She wants to know what you're doing, when you're doing it, and who you're doing it with. And once you've told her, watch out, because that's when the critique and commentary begin!

Moms are our biggest cheerleaders; they want nothing more than to see us succeed. But Mom will always think of you as her baby, and she will make sure you're equipped to deal with any challenge that comes your way. She has advice for everything, and she will drop her knowledge on you whether you want it or not. She's had a lifetime to learn what she knows, and she's happy to take up your lifetime passing it along, no matter how old you are, or how well things are going.

A mom's delivery can be forward, funny, and sometimes downright fresh. Some moms sugar-coat their wisdom; others go straight for the jugular. But all Mom wants to do is make you a better person. And if that means knocking you down a peg, so be it! No mother is afraid of showing her child tough love.

While getting "mothered" as a child is part of routine everyday life, and getting lectured as a teenager can be downright frustrating, talking to your mother as an adult can be one of life's greatest pleasures. Your Mom no longer sees the need to be coy with you or show any parental pretense—she's ready to speak the truth she thinks you need to hear.

And her sense of humor will come out in ways you never thought possible! When your mother starts to speak to you as an adult, you get some of the most colorful, vivid language imaginable. She won't "work blue" like Dad might, but she can turn a phrase that will keep you laughing or leave you speechless with her withering rebuke.

This book is a collection of some of the best replies, retorts, and repartee from multiple generations of moms. Some of these lines of motherly advice and words of wisdom will be new to you, while others will be amusingly familiar. Covering a range of topics from fashion and careers to relationships, hygiene, and beyond, these quips and quotes will keep you smiling. And who knows, the next time *your* Mom calls, you'll be armed and ready for whatever grief and guidance she's ready to dispense.

1.

IT'S JUST MOM BEING MOM...

JEFF:

Hi, Mom, how are you?

MOM:

Not good, I haven't eaten in days.

JEFF:

Why haven't you eaten?

MOM:

*Because I didn't want my mouth
to be full in case you called.*

ADAM:

*You know, when I have my own place, I won't
have to live by these dumb rules.*

MOM:

*Oh, for Pete's sake! You have a mouth like a
pistol—you're always shooting it off.*

MOM:

Which one of you broke that?

FINN:

It was Sally!

SALLY:

No, it was Finn!

MOM:

I can't believe I gave birth to two wild animals. I should have left you at the zoo when I had the chance.

Hi, Mom, how are you?

I'm good, darling, what are you up to?

Not much, just hanging out with the guys. What's up?

Well, I thought of you all day today. I was at the zoo.

MOM...? MOM...? MOM!

I'm busy now.
Can I ignore you some other time?

. . . .

What are you boys doing in there,
making all that noise?

NOTHING...

Well, if you have nothing to do,
don't do it here!

MOM:

Hi, honey, are you sick?

ANNA:

No, why?

MOM:

Then why don't you pick up the phone when I call?

....

MOM:

Eat your dinner. You know, there are people starving in Africa.

DANIEL:

Fine then, they can have it instead.

MOM:

Honey, you don't have enough brains to be a smartass, you're just being an ass.

MOM:
What are you doing for the bachelor party?

BRO:
We're going to a steak-house and a strip club.

MOM:
Well, at least mind your manners.

SIS:
I've never been to a strip club.

MOM:
Be careful or you'll end up on the pole!

KATE:
There's no Wi-Fi in here?!

TODD:
Yeah, why did you pick this place, Mom?

KATE:
I'm going to give them a horrible Yelp review.

MOM:
Listen to me: just because you have an asshole doesn't mean you have to act like one.

NEIL:

Sorry I forgot your birthday, Mom. I just had so much going on at work...

MOM:

Wipe your mouth, darling, there's still a tiny bit of bullshit around your lips.

MOM:
What activities are you doing this school year?

BRO:
I'm playing football and hockey.

MOM:
That sounds like fun. And you?

SIS:
I'm doing dance and field hockey.

MOM:
Oh my god, you'll get killed!

MOM:
Oh, look, it's Mr. and Mrs. Zimmerman.

BRO:
Geez, she's so fat!

MOM:
Now stop that, that's not very nice.

SIS:
And he's so short!

MOM:
I know, right?

SIS:

Mom, can I get a ride?

MOM:

Why don't you get a ride
from your brother?

SIS:

He went out for a drive.
Why can't I get a car?

MOM:

No daughter of mine is going
joyriding alone!

*Darling, are you and your husband ever
going to have a baby?*

I DON'T KNOW.
SOMEDAY,
MAYBE. WHY?

*Before I die I'd like to hold something
cute besides your miniature dog.*

2.

MOM ON BAD HABITS...

What are you doing? Are you drinking milk straight from the carton?

Um, yeah. Sorry, Mom.

How did you get here? Did someone leave your cage open?

We had a big frat party on Saturday night. Until the cops showed up, anyway.

You make a fantastic bad example

Who left the leftovers out?

Sorry, that was me.

I could smack you right now, but
that would be animal abuse.

AND WHERE WERE YOU LADIES LAST NIGHT?

Oh, we just went to the movies.

I CAN ALWAYS TELL WHEN YOU'RE LYING. YOUR LIPS MOVE.

BRO:

Can I have some wine at dinner tonight?

MOM:

Well, I suppose. I don't want to insult our hosts.

SIS:

What about me?

MOM:

What? Good girls don't drink!

....

MEGAN:

I just bought a new phone.

MOM:

Another one?! You go through money like your father goes through antacids.

MOM:

What did you do last night?

BRO:

Went out with the guys.
Baxter was drunk and
hit on girls.

MOM:

I want to hear all about it.
And how about you?

SIS:

Molly got drunk, too. She
was a mess.

MOM:

Now, sweetie, you know
I've never liked her.

MOM:
What did you guys do last night?

SIS:
I watched a bunch of movies on TV.

MOM:
That sounds like fun! And you?

BRO:
I played video games for like four hours.

MOM:
You have a problem, mister!

What is all that buzzing noise?

OH, IT'S MY PHONE.
I'M TEXTING
MY GIRLFRIEND.

*Every time I'm with you, I get a
fierce desire to be alone.*

. . . .

*Why don't you have a shirt on,
young man?*

I DIDN'T FEEL LIKE
PUTTING ONE ON.

*As an outsider, what do you
think of the human race?*

You're on that
phone 24 hours a
day, but somehow
you never call
your mother.

MOM:

Where are you two going?

BRO:

I'm heading over to Randy's house.

MOM:

I know what you boys do there. Promise
me you won't drink and drive.

SIS:

I'm going to Amelia's house.

MOM:

No drinking!

ISABELLA:

Mom, what's with you and '80s music?

MOM:

I grew up in the '80s!

ISABELLA:

I still don't know why you love it so much.

MOM:

You know what I love about the '80s? I didn't have to look at your selfies.

MOM:

Why are you home so early?

KYLE:

We got kicked out of the mall for loitering.

MOM:

Ordinarily people live and learn.
You just live.

....

MOM:

Who put an empty container of
juice back in the fridge?

ERIC:

Oh, I guess I did that.

MOM:

If they gave you an IQ test the results
would be negative.

Did you
remember
to flush?

MOM:

Well, you're up early.

SIS:

I couldn't sleep. I only got about six hours.

MOM:

Honey, that's not good for your health. You've got to get more sleep. And where's your brother?

SIS:

He's still in bed.

MOM:

That lazy, good-for-nothing...

SIS:

I'm leaving, Mom!

MOM:

*If you're not back by 10:00, you're grounded,
young lady!*

SIS:

Don't worry, I'll be home...

BRO:

I'm heading out, too, Mom.

MOM:

And you—don't you come home too drunk!

My friend is acting all weird. She's such a jerk sometimes.

If you're gonna be two-faced, honey, at least make one of them pretty.

My friend got a new tattoo—and it's misspelled.

If she had two brains she would be twice as dumb.

3.

MOM ON FASHION...

What are you wearing?

Me and the guys are going out to try and meet some girls.

Well, whatever kind of look you were aiming for, you missed.

What do you think of this romper, Mom?

I love that you're not afraid to be yourself.

ROMEO:
Hey, Mom—I'm going on a date.
How's my outfit?

MOM:
You look great. Except for your clothes.

CHUCK:
Mom, what did you do with my old
workout t-shirt?

MOM:
I took it to Goodwill, and
Goodwill sent it back.

MOM:
What are you wearing?

SIS:
Just some jeans and a nice blouse.

MOM:
No, you're not! Go upstairs and put on something nice. Now what about you?

BRO:
I dunno. I guess these jeans and an Oxford shirt.

MOM:
Well...at least tuck in your shirt.

KAREN:

How did I look last night?

MOM:

You looked great—I didn't even recognize you!

....

LESLIE:

Do you like my new shorts?

MOM:

Your keister must be hungry because it's always eating your shorts.

OH, MOM, COME HERE— WHAT DO YOU THINK OF THIS BLOUSE?

That's a nice shirt, sweetheart, what brand is it? Clearance?

Is that what you're wearing out, young man?

YEAH, I JUST THREW ON A SWEATSHIRT AND SOME JEANS.

It's refreshing to meet someone who doesn't care how they look.

ELAINE:

I just found the cutest outfit at the store!

MOM:

Well even a blind squirrel finds a nut once in a while.

WHAT DO YOU THINK OF THIS JUMPSUIT, MOM?

I think it makes you look ugly.

MOM! STOP INSULTING ME!

I'm not insulting you. I'm describing you.

....

I DON'T KNOW, MOM. IS THIS SHIRT A LITTLE TOO REVEALING?

Sweetheart, it's okay to be easy, just as long as you're not cheap.

4.

THE SASSY MOM...

NATHAN:
My friends and I are going to an EDM concert.

MOM:
Now I understand why some animals eat their young.

LEON:
I forgot to water my plants, so now they're all dead.

MOM:
You're impossible to underestimate.

I cannot figure out what's wrong with my car!

Oh, sweetie, I'm so glad you're pretty.

My buddies and I are joining a dodgeball league.

I always feel smarter after talking with you.

MATT:
The good news is, I got a B on my physics final!

MOM:
See! You aren't as dumb as you look!

GARY:
Mom, you've seen me— I'm a pretty awesome dancer, right?

MOM:
I could agree with you, but then we'd both be wrong.

OUR TEAM CAME IN FIRST PLACE IN THE INTRAMURAL SOFTBALL LEAGUE.

You should be proud of that. It's the best thing you'll ever do.

MOM:

What happened to your foot?

TIMMY:

I was seeing how high I could throw a brick in the air.

MOM:

Are you always this thick, or is today a special occasion?

MOM:

Why is your face so flushed?

BOBBY:

I was seeing how long I could hold my breath.

MOM:

Everyone is entitled to a dumb moment, but you abuse the privilege.

MY ROOMMATE IS REALLY INTO AROMATHERAPY.

Oh, bless her heart.

I'VE DECIDED I'M GOING TO GET RID OF SOME OF MY OLD DOLLS AND STUFFED ANIMALS.

*You're starting to sound reasonable.
It must be time to up my medication!*

MADISON:

Mom, I need a new phone. This one's so old it barely even works anymore.

MOM:

Sorry, I didn't hear you. I don't speak bullshit.

How big is the specific ocean?

The what?

The specific ocean. How big is it?

If you were any dumber, someone would have to water you twice a week.

Where are my garbage bags?

We jumped off the roof and used them as parachutes.

Did you eat paint chips when
you were a baby?

Where is your brother?

HE'S TRYING TO WASH THE MAGIC MARKER OFF HIS FACE.

That boy is as sharp as a bowling ball.

ALEX:

Hey, Mom?

MOM:

Yes.

ALEX:

Does every religion
celebrate Thanksgiving?

MOM:

Cheese and rice! You're
depriving some poor
village of its idiot.

5.

MOM ON
RELATIONSHIPS...

I MET THIS REALLY WEIRD GUY ON TINDER.

*If there was a nutjob within
50 miles they'd find you.*

MOM:

So...what's happening with the boys?

SIS:

Nothing, really. I'm just focusing on school.

MOM:

Well, there must be someone you like?

SIS:

Why are you asking me? Mark's had plenty of girlfriends.

MOM:

Yes, but I don't want to pry into his private life.

MOM:

Who are you going
to the wedding
with, dear?

ALLISON:

No one. I'm just
going by myself.

MOM:

You're so
independent,
no wonder you
haven't found
anyone yet.

MOM:

What are you doing on your date, kiddo?

MARIA:

He's taking me out for dinner.

MOM:

Well you better learn to cook, because it takes face powder to catch a man, but baking powder to keep him.

I MET A NICE GUY, HE'S A CONSULTANT FOR A TECH COMPANY.

If he's a consultant, it means he hasn't had a job in five years.

MOM:
What are you two talking about?

BRO:
Sam cheated on his girlfriend.

MOM:
Well, that's disgusting. He should be ashamed.

SIS:
And Emily cheated on her boyfriend.

MOM:
Oh my! What did he do wrong?

MOM:

*Why don't you have a
girlfriend yet?*

BRO:

*I don't know. It just hasn't
worked out.*

MOM:

But you're such a handsome boy.

SIS:

*I have a crush on someone
at school.*

MOM:

*You're not allowed to date
until you're 50!*

My roommate has dated three different guys this week.

If she were an escort, at least she'd be an expensive one.

BRO:

Mom, is it okay if my girlfriend comes over?

MOM:

Yes, but please hang out down in the basement.

BRO:

But Julie's down there with her boyfriend.

MOM:

What? Julie! Get up here right this minute!

WHY IS IT SO HARD TO FIND A RELATIONSHIP? WHAT AM I DOING WRONG?

They say opposites attract. I hope you meet someone who's intelligent and cultured.

....

I'M DATING DYLAN AGAIN.

What? I thought you broke up.

WE DID, BUT HE'S DIFFERENT NOW!

Listen, I may love to shop, but I'm not buying your BS.

6.

WHAT DO YOU THINK?

WHAT DO YOU THINK I AM, YOUR PERSONAL MAID?

What do you think I am, your personal bank?

What do you think I am, your personal chef?

What do you think I am, a taxi service?

What do you think I am, a cleaning lady?

What do you think I am, a waitress?

**What do you think I am,
a mind-reader?**

....

**What do you think I am,
made of money?**

....

**What do you think this is,
a restaurant?**

....

**What do you think this is,
a rooming house?**

....

**What do you think this is,
a charity?**

What, do you think we live in a barn?

What do you think this is, some kind of joke?

7.

MOM ON GROOMING...

Mom, what do you think of my bangs?

You'd be perfect for one of those makeover shows.

Mom, is this too much lipstick?

Usually girls who wear that much makeup have something to hide, but you pull it off.

Wow, your hair and makeup look great!

THANKS, MOM!

You look so nice when you put a little effort into your appearance!

MOM:

What in the world happened to your hair?

FRANKIE:

I tried to cut it by myself.

MOM:

If genius skips a generation, your children will be brilliant.

SWEETIE, WHO DID YOUR MAKEUP, PICASSO?

I JUST HAD A FACIAL AND GOT MY EYEBROWS WAXED.

You know, nothing on your face is particularly pretty, but somehow it all just works together.

. . . .

What is that mess, mister?

I JUST CAME FROM THE BARBER. I'M TRYING OUT A NEW LOOK.

Did you get a bowl of soup with that haircut?

Mom, what do you think of my new hairstyle?

Honey, you're supposed to look better in the "after" picture.

MOM, DO I NEED TO PUT ON ANY MORE MAKEUP?

Maybe if you ate all that makeup instead of plastering it on your face, you'd at least be pretty on the inside.

8.

THE SHARP-TONGUED MOM...

KAYLEE:
Oh my God, what a day. The power went out and I was trapped on an escalator for a half-hour.

MOM:
An escalator?

KAYLEE:
Yeah. And I barely had cellphone reception.

MOM:
Listen, honey, it's better to let someone think you're an idiot than to open your mouth and prove it.

MOM:

Why is the dog wearing a sweater?

LANA:

To keep him warm.

MOM:

So, what's his fur for?

LANA:

I don't know. It's like his hair, I guess.

MOM:

Well, there's no vaccine against stupidity.

MY BUDDIES AND I ARE THINKING ABOUT INSTALLING A FIRE POLE IN OUR HOUSE.

You boys are the reason the gene pool needs a lifeguard.

RYAN:

So now I can't find my wallet...

MOM:

*I am so glad natural selection
is no longer a factor.*

My roommate is really into crystal healing.

She's so open-minded her brains have fallen out.

Mom, why aren't there any photos of George Washington?

I can explain it to you, son, but I can't understand it for you.

Mom, I broke your tennis racket. I was using it as an air guitar.

Calling you dumb would be an insult to all the stupid people.

JESS:

It's like I can't even do math without my phone anymore.

MOM:

Well, brains aren't everything. In your case, they're nothing.

BRIANNA:

I've been thinking about becoming a vegan.

MOM:

I am so jealous of people that don't know you...

PHIL:

So I was thinking, if I go to bed one hour earlier each day this week, I won't have any jetlag when I fly to Europe.

MOM:

Good gravy! You have diarrhea of the mouth and a constipation of ideas.

MOM:
How did you rip
your pants?

SEAN:
I was break-dancing
at a football
tailgate.

MOM:
It's scary to think
that people like
you are graduating
from college.

ISAAC:

Hey, Mom, Ally and I are renting a car. How far is the drive from San Diego to California?

MOM:

¡Ay, caramba! 100,000 sperm, and you were the fastest?

ALEX:

*Hey, Mom, do people with blue eyes
see everything tinted blue?*

MOM:

*Oh, honey, do you ever wonder what life would
be like if you'd had enough oxygen at birth?*

Hey, sweetie, why are you getting all dolled up?

THERE'S THIS CUTE NEW FRENCH EXCHANGE STUDENT AT SCHOOL. HE'S LIKE, FROM ROME OR SOMETHING.

If only they sold brains in the makeup aisle.

OLIVIA:

Hey, Mom, what's a naturalized citizen? Is that someone who wasn't born in a test tube?

MOM:

What? Are you kidding me?

OLIVIA:

Am I a naturalized citizen?

MOM:

You must have been born on a highway because that's where most accidents happen.

ETHAN:

You know, if you blink fast enough, life looks like one of those old-timey movies.

MOM:

Darling, if there was a single intelligent thought in your head, it would have died from loneliness.

I GOT ASKED TO BE A BRIDESMAID AGAIN.

It always shocks me that so many people like you.

9.

MOM ON HOMEMAKING...

There's enough dirt in
this place to grow
potatoes!

If you two are going to
kill each other, do
it outside—I just
finished cleaning!

Young man, you need to make this bed!

WHY SHOULD I MAKE MY BED WHEN I'M JUST GOING TO SLEEP IN IT TONIGHT?

Why eat when you're just going to die anyway?

LAURIE:
Mom, what did you think of the dessert I made?

MOM:
It was good! I had no idea you could make something like that from a box.

OWEN:
My new apartment has a nice view!

MOM:
If only you could see it through those dirty windows.

MOM:
What's everybody having for dinner?

SIS:
I'm grilling some asparagus, fingerling potatoes, and marinated chicken.

MOM:
Hmmm.

BRO:
I made pasta and some jar sauce.

MOM:
Well, look at my little chef!

Did you finally clean up that pigsty
of a room, mister?

YES, MOM.

Good. And keep rolling your eyes, maybe
you'll find your brain back there.

MOM:
Okay, I need you to take out the garbage and mow the lawn.

BRO:
Oh, man. Right now?

MOM:
Yes, right now! Do you think the garbage is going to take itself out?

SIS:
I can take it out.

MOM:
Oh, don't worry, it's not that important.

JENNIFER:

Mom, what are you doing?

MOM:

I'm sweeping your floor.

JENNIFER:

Why? It's just a little dust!

MOM:

Your house is so filthy you have to wipe your feet before you go outside.

What is that smell? Did someone die in here?

O.

MOM ON CAREERS & AMBITIONS....

SALLY:
I think I'd like to take a month off from work and travel the world.

MOM:
Darling, I'll always love you and support you...despite your choices!

———————————

MOM:
Let's see those report cards...

BRO:
I got a C in biology.

MOM:
Well, you gave it your best effort.

SIS:
I got a B in physics.

MOM:
Oh, darling, you can do better than that!

I'VE DECIDED TO QUIT COLLEGE AND START A BAND.

Honey, I need you to do me a favor.

WHAT'S THAT?

I want you to be a pallbearer at my funeral so you can let me down one last time.

. . . .

SCOTT:

I just wish I could get a better job.

MOM:

Wish in one hand and shit in the other and see which one fills up the fastest.

YOU'RE SO SMART, WHY ARE YOU STUDYING ART?

. . . .

MOM:

And how is school going, kiddo?

JERRY:

Fine. I signed up for a few easy classes this semester.

MOM:

In a country where anyone can be anything, I'll never understand why you choose to be mediocre.

BRO:
I think I'd like to get an MBA at
some point.

MOM:
That shows a lot of ambition.

SIS:
I'd like to get a doctorate.

MOM:
And when will you ever get a husband?

SETH:
I'd love to become an astronaut.
Meeting aliens would be cool.

MOM:
Don't you love nature, despite what it
did to you?

BRO:
I think I'm going to apply for a job at
the gas station.

MOM:
That's very industrious of you!

SIS:
Maybe I should apply.

MOM:
And be surrounded by all those
disgusting strangers?

MOM:
Oh, look at my beautiful, intelligent daughter.
Someday you'll be a doctor or lawyer.

SIS:
Thanks, Mom.

BRO:
What about me, Mom?

MOM:
You'll figure something out.

CLINT:

I'm thinking about majoring in sociology.

MOM:

Why don't you learn to drive a bus, so you'll have something to fall back on?

SHAUNA:
I'm auditioning for a role
at the regional theater.

MOM:
It's good not to dream
too big!

PETER:
I'd like to become a body
builder, that would be
totally cool.

MOM:
I fully support you in your
fight against reality.

TOM:

I was thinking I would take some time off from school, maybe go camping for a few weeks out in the desert, and really just find myself.

MOM:

Funny how your mind is on vacation, but your mouth is working overtime.

....

AMANDA:

I just switched my major again.

MOM:

You're a jack of all trades, and a master of none.

1.

MOM ON BODY IMAGE...

Oh, now what are those new clothes?

I JUST GOT THIS SUIT BACK FROM THE TAILOR. WHAT DO YOU THINK?

Most of your clothes make you look fat, but those don't.

CAROL:

Ugh, this sweater doesn't even fit me anymore.

MOM:

Remember, the only thing attractive about a muffin top is the name.

SIS:
Gwen broke up with her boyfriend.

MOM:
Well, he wasn't much of a looker anyway.

BRO:
Are you kidding? Gwen's no model either!

MOM:
Oh, don't be so shallow!

You're so beautiful when you smile, princess, you should do it more.

If you didn't have feet you wouldn't wear shoes, so why do you wear a bra?

MOM:
You look good, what happened?

ASHLEY:
What do you mean?

MOM:
You're so thin! Have you been sick?

AMY:
I hate how I look in that picture.

MOM:
How much better do you think you look in real life?

MOM:
Why are you so sweaty?

SIS:
I was at the gym. I'm trying to tone up.

MOM:
Honey, girls shouldn't have muscles. Boys should have muscles, which is too bad for your brother.

BRO:
We're heading to the beach, Mom.

MOM:
Well, look at you, Mr. Muscles. Don't you look buff in your swimsuit?

SIS:
Have you seen my sunglasses?

MOM:
Oh geez, sweetheart, you really should cover up that bikini!

MOM, DID YOU SEE THE PICTURES FROM MY GIRLS' WEEKEND?

Yes, you look so pretty on your Instagram. Did you use filters or something?

....

IF I CAN'T GET A JOB, I'M GOING TO HAVE TO SELL MY BODY.

With a body like that? You'd be lucky to get a nickel.

About Cider Mill Press Book Publishers

Good ideas ripen with time. From seed to harvest, Cider Mill
Press brings fine reading, information, and entertainment
together between the covers of its creatively crafted books.
Our Cider Mill bears fruit twice a year, publishing
a new crop of titles each spring and fall.

**BOOK
PUBLISHERS**
KENNEBUNKPORT, MAINE

"Where Good Books Are Ready for Press"

Visit us online at
cidermillpress.com
or write to us at
PO Box 454
12 Spring St.
Kennebunkport, Maine 04046